I0811073

THE SECRET OF FELLOWSHIP

THE SECRET OF
FELLOWSHIP

Andrew Murray

CLC PUBLICATIONS
Fort Washington, PA 19034

The Secret of Fellowship
Published by CLC Publications

U.S.A.
P.O. Box 1449, Fort Washington, PA 19034

UNITED KINGDOM
CLC International (UK)
Unit 5, Glendale Avenue, Sandycroft, Flintshire, CH5 2QP

© 1998 CLC Publications
All rights reserved
This printing 2019

Printed in the United States of America

ISBN (paperback): 978-1-61958-298-9
ISBN (e-book): 978-1-61958-299-6

Unless otherwise noted, all Scripture quotations are from the Holy Bible, New King James Version, copyright © 1979, 1980, 1982 by Thomas Nelson, Inc. Used by permission. All rights reserved.

Scripture quotations marked ASV are from the Holy Bible, American Standard Version, 1901.

Italics in Scripture quotations are the emphasis of the author.

Cover design by Mitch Bolton.

INTRODUCTION

To my Brethren in the Ministry:

BELOVED brethren—The more I think of and pray about the state of religion in this country and all over the world, the deeper my conviction becomes that the low state of the spiritual life of Christians is due to the fact that they do not realize that the aim and object of conversion is to bring the soul, even here on earth, *to a daily fellowship with the Father in heaven.* When once this truth has been accepted, the believer will perceive how indispensable it is to the spiritual life of a Christian to take time each day with God's Word, and, in prayer, to wait upon God for His presence and His love to be revealed.

But how can Christians be taught this lesson and be persuaded to live in obedience to it? The first thing is that the minister *himself* must be convinced of the great need for daily fellowship with God and must grasp his calling to train his people to habits of prayer. His hearers must be brought under the impression, through his preaching, that it is not enough at conversion to accept forgiveness of sins or even to surrender themselves to God. That is only a beginning. The young believer must understand that he has no power of his own to maintain his spiritual life.

No, he needs each day to receive new grace from heaven through fellowship with the Lord Jesus. This cannot be obtained by a hasty prayer or a superficial reading of a few verses from God's Word. He must take time quietly and deliberately to come into God's presence, to feel his weakness and his need, and to wait upon God through His Holy Spirit to renew the heavenly light and life in his heart. Then he may rightly expect to be kept by the power of Christ throughout the day, through all its temptations.

It has been my aim in writing this little book to help Christians to see the absolute necessity of fellowship with the Lord Jesus. Without this, the joy and power of God's Holy Spirit in daily life cannot be experienced. Many of God's children long for a better life but do not realize the need of giving God time day by day in the inner chamber to renew and sanctify their lives by His Spirit. Oh, that every minister would lead and help those under his charge to grasp this great truth.

Beloved brethren, meditate on this thought: *The feeble state of my spiritual life is mainly due to the lack of time day by day in fellowship with God.* The minister is the one who must teach this lesson to his people, and encourage them to believe that a different life is possible. New life will dawn in many a soul as a result of time spent in prayer alone with God.

If you should find a blessing in reading this little book, I ask that you share the blessing with others. If you have accepted the message that the Lord Jesus will, day by day, grant you His presence and love, pass it on to others. However weak and impotent you feel, your faith will be strengthened as you help others to realize their need of fellowship with Jesus daily.

As we think of the need of our country and church, as we think of souls around us, as we think of the extension of God's kingdom, we ask you, O Christians, to help us find volunteers, who, as true soldiers of the cross, will persevere continually in prayer till God pours out His blessing upon us.

Your servant in the love of Christ and in prayer,

ANDREW MURRAY
Wellington, South Africa

Day 1

Day by Day

The inward man is being renewed day by day.
Second Corinthians 4:16

THERE is one lesson that all young Christians should learn, namely this: *the absolute necessity of fellowship with Jesus each day.* This lesson is not always taught at the beginning of the Christian life, nor is it always understood by the young convert. He should realize that the grace he has received of the forgiveness of sins, of acceptance as God's child, of joy in the Holy Spirit, can only be preserved by the daily renewal of fellowship with Jesus Christ Himself.

Many Christians backslide because this truth is not clearly taught. They are unable to stand against the temptations of the world or of their old nature. They strive to do their best to fight against sin and to serve God, but they have no strength. They have never really grasped the secret: The Lord Jesus will *every day* from heaven continue His work in me. But on one condition—*the soul must give Him time each day* to impart His love and His grace. Time alone with the Lord Jesus each day is the indispensable condition of growth and power.

Read Matthew 11:25–30. Listen to Christ's word: "Come to Me . . . and I will give you rest. . . . Learn from Me . . . and you will find rest for your souls" (Matt. 11:28–29). The Lord will teach us just how gentle and humble He is. Bow before Him, tell Him that you long for Him and His love, and He will let His love rest on you.

This is a thought not only for young Christians but for all who love the Lord, and this little book is designed to help those who desire to live this life of fellowship with Christ. We will try to put the message as clearly, as lovingly, as urgently as possible. May each of us start with this resolve: For the sake of Christ, and in order to please Him; for my own sake, and to enable me to enjoy this blessed experience each day, I will learn the lesson to *spend time each day*—without exception—*in fellowship with my Lord.* So will our inner man be renewed day by day.

Day 2

Fellowship with God

As the Father loved Me, I also have loved you; abide in My love.

John 15:9

THE three Persons in the Godhead are the Father, the Son, and the Holy Spirit. Each One knows Himself as distinct from the others. God desires to reveal Himself as a Person. Each one of us is an individual, knowing himself as distinct from others and standing in certain relationships to others. God will reveal Himself to us as a Person, and it is our holy calling to enter into fellowship with Him.

God greatly desires this intimacy with man. But sin has come between man and his God. Even in the Christian who thinks he knows God, there is often great ignorance and even indifference to this personal relationship of love to God. People believe that at conversion their sins are forgiven, that God accepts them so that they may go to heaven, and that they should try to do God's will. But the idea is strange to them that even as a father and his child on earth have pleasure in companionship, *so they may and must each day have this blessed fellowship with God.*

God gave Christ His Son to *bring us to Himself.* But this is only possible when we live in close fellowship with Jesus Christ. Our relationship to Christ rests on His deep, tender love to us. We are not able of ourselves to render Him this love, but the Holy Spirit will do the work in us. For this we need to separate ourselves each day from the world and turn in faith to the Lord Jesus, that He may pour out His love in our hearts *so that we may be filled with a great love to Him.*

Dear soul, meditate quietly on this thought. Read the words of Christ in John 14:21, "He who loves Me will be loved by My Father, and I will love him." Take time to believe in this personal fellowship. Tell Him of your love. Say to Him: "Lord, You have loved me dearly; most earnestly do I desire to love You above all."

Day 3

Jesus

You shall call His name Jesus, for He will save His people from their sins.

Matthew 1:21

AS the Lord Jesus was a person, He had His own individual name. His mother, His disciples, all His friends called Him by this name—Jesus. But they probably thought little of what that name meant. And how little do the majority of Christians know what a treasure is contained in that name Jesus: "*He will save His people from their sins.*"

Many think of His death on the cross; they think of His work in heaven as Intercessor; but do they or we realize that He is a living person in heaven, one who thinks of us each day and longs to reveal Himself? And He desires us each day to bring Him our love and adoration.

Christians pray to Christ to save them from their sins, but they know very little how the blessed work is done. The living Christ reveals Himself to us and through the power of His love the love of sin is expelled. It is *through personal fellowship* with Him that Jesus saves from our sins. I must come as an individual, with my heart and all the sin that is in it, to Jesus as an almighty personal Savior in whom God's holiness dwells. And as He and I commune together in the expression of mutual love and desire, by the work of His

Holy Spirit in my heart His love will expel and conquer all the sin.

O Christian, learn the blessedness of each day in fellowship with Jesus finding the secret of happiness and holiness. Your heart will long for the hour of prayer as the best hour of the day. As you learn to go apart with Him alone each day, you will experience His presence with you, enabling you all through the day to love Him, to serve Him, and to walk in His ways. Through this unbroken fellowship you will learn the secret of the power of a truly godly life.

Day 4

The Inner Chamber

When thou prayest, enter into thine inner chamber.

Matthew 6:6, ASV

HAVE you ever thought what a wonderful privilege it is that every one each day—and each hour of the day—has the liberty of asking God to meet him in the inner chamber and to hear what he has to say? We should imagine that every Christian would use such a privilege gladly and faithfully.

"When you pray," says Jesus, "go into your room, and when you have shut your door, pray to your Father who is in the secret place" (6:6). That means two things. Shut the world *out,* withdraw from all worldly thoughts and occupations; and shut yourself *in* alone with God, to pray to Him in secret. Let this be your chief object in prayer, to *realize the presence of your heavenly Father.* Let your watchword be: alone with God.

This is only the beginning. I must take time to realize His presence with me, and pray to my Father who sees in secret in the full assurance that He knows how I long for His help and guidance, and will incline His ear to me.

Then follows the great promise: "Your Father who sees in secret will reward you openly" (6:6). My Father will see to it that my prayer is not in vain. All through the occupations of a busy day the answer to my prayer will be granted. *Prayer in secret will be followed by the secret working of God in my heart.*

As the Lord Jesus has given us the promise of His presence and shows us the way to the inner chamber, He will assuredly be with us to teach us to pray. It is through Him that we have access to the Father. Be childlike and trustful in your fellowship with Christ. Confess each sin; bring your every need. Offer your prayer to the Father in the name of Christ. *Prayer in fellowship with Jesus* cannot be in vain.

Day 5

Faith

Only believe.

Mark 5:36

WE have here a lesson of the greatest importance, namely this: that when alone in the inner chamber we must send up our petitions trusting implicitly in the love of God and in the power of the Lord Jesus. Take time to ask yourself the question: "Is my heart full of a great and steadfast faith in God's love?" If this is not the case, do not begin to pray at once. Faith does not come of itself. Consider quietly how impossible it is for God to lie. He is ready with infinite love to give you a blessing. Take some text of Scripture in which God's power and faithfulness and love are revealed. Appropriate the words, and say: "Yes, Lord, I will pray in firm faith in You and in Your great love."

It is a mistake to limit the word "faith" to the forgiveness of sins and our acceptance as children of God. Faith includes far more. We must have faith *in all that God is willing to do for us*. We must have faith each day according to our special needs. God is infinitely great and powerful. And Christ has so much grace for each new day that our faith must reach out afresh each day according to the need of the day.

When you enter into the inner chamber, even before you begin to pray, ask yourself: "Do I really believe that *God is here with me*, and that *the Lord Jesus will help me to pray*, so I may expect to spend a blessed time in communion with my God?"

Jesus often taught His disciples how indispensable faith was to true prayer. He will teach us this lesson too. Remain in fellowship with Him, and ask Him to strengthen your faith in His almighty power. Christ says to you and to me as to Martha: "Did I not say to you that if you would believe you would see the glory of God?" (John 11:40).

Day 6

The Word of God

Man shall not live by bread alone, but by every word that proceeds from the mouth of God.

Matthew 4:4

THE illustration that our Lord uses, in which the Word of God is compared to our daily bread, is most instructive.

Bread is indispensable to life. We all understand this. However strong a person may be, if he takes no nourishment he will grow weaker and life will become extinct. Even so with the Word of God. It contains a heavenly principle and works powerfully in those who believe.

Bread must be eaten. I may know all about bread. I may have bread and may give it to others. I may have bread in my house and on my table in great abundance, but that will not help me; if through illness I am unable to eat it, I shall die. And so a mere knowledge of God's Word—and even the preaching of it to others—will not avail me. It is not enough just to think about it; I must feed on God's Word and take it into my heart and life. In love and obedience I must appropriate the words of God, must let them take full possession of my heart. Then they will indeed be words of life.

Bread must be eaten daily. And the same is true of God's Word. The psalmist says: "Blessed is the man / . . . [whose] delight is in the law of the LORD, / And *in His law he meditates day and night*" (Ps. 1:1–2); "Oh, how

I love Your law! / It is my meditation *all the day*" (Ps. 119:97). To secure a strong and powerful spiritual life God's Word every day is indispensable.

When on earth, the Lord Jesus learned, loved, and obeyed the word of the Father. And if you seek fellowship with Him, you will find Him in His Word. Christ will teach you to commune with the Father through the Word, even as was His custom. You will learn, like Him, to live solely for the glory of God and the fulfillment of His Word.

Day 7

How to Read God's Word

Blessed is the man . . . [whose] delight is in the law of the L*ORD*, *And in His law he meditates day and night.*

Psalm 1:1–2

HERE are some simple rules for Bible reading. *Read God's Word with great reverence.* Meditate a moment in silence on the thought that the words come from God Himself. Bow in deep reverence. Be silent before the Lord. Let Him reveal His Word in your heart.

Read with careful attention. If you read the words carelessly, thinking that you can grasp their meaning with your human understanding, you will use the words superficially and not enter into their depths. When someone tries to explain anything wonderful or beautiful to us, we give our entire attention to try to understand what is said. How much higher and deeper are God's thoughts than our thoughts. "As the heavens are higher than the earth, / So are My ways higher than your ways, / And My thoughts than your thoughts" (Isa. 55:9). We need to give our undivided attention to understand even the superficial meaning of the words. How much harder one should attempt to grasp the spiritual meaning.

Read with the expectation of the guidance of God's Spirit. It is God's Spirit alone who can make the Word a living power in our hearts and lives. Read Psalm 119.

Notice how earnestly David prays that God will teach him, and open his eyes, and give him understanding, and incline his heart to God's ways. As you read, remember that God's Word and God's Spirit are inseparable.

Read with the firm purpose of keeping the Word day and night in your heart and in your life. The whole heart and the whole life must come under the influence of the Word. David said: "Oh, how I love Your law! / It is my meditation all the day" (Ps. 119:97). And so in the midst of his daily work, the believer can cherish God's Word in his heart and meditate on it. Read Psalm 119 again, until you accept God's Word with all your heart, and pray that God may teach you to understand it and to carry out its precepts in your life.

Day 8

The Word and Prayer

Revive me, O Lord, according to Your word.

Psalm 119:107

PRAYER and the Word of God are inseparable, and should always go together in the quiet time of the inner chamber. *In His Word God speaks to me; in prayer I speak to God.* If there is to be true communication, God and I must both take part. If I simply pray, without using God's Word, I am apt to use my own words and thoughts. But here is what really gives prayer its power—that I take God's thoughts from His Word and present them before Him. Then I am enabled to pray according to God's Word. How indispensable God's Word is for all true prayer!

When I pray, I must seek to know God aright. It is through the Word that the Holy Spirit gives me right thoughts about Him. The Word will also teach me how wretched and sinful I am. It reveals to me all the wonders that God will do for me, and the strength He will give me to do His Will. The Word teaches me how to pray—with strong desire, with a firm faith, and with constant perseverance. The Word teaches me not only what I am but what I may become through God's grace. And above all, it reminds me each day that Christ is the great Intercessor and allows me to pray in His name.

O Christian, learn this great lesson: *I must renew my strength each day in God's Word, that I might pray according to His will.*

Then we turn to the other side—prayer. We need prayer when we read God's Word—prayer to be taught by God to understand His Word, prayer that through the Holy Spirit I may rightly know and use God's Word, prayer that I may see in the Word that Christ is all in all and will be all in me.

Blessed inner chamber, where I may approach God in Christ through the Word and prayer. There I may offer myself to God and His service and be strengthened by the Holy Spirit so that His love may be poured out in my heart and I may daily walk in that love.

Day 9

Obedience

Obey My voice . . . and I will be your God.

Jeremiah 11:4

GOD gave this command to Israel when He gave them the law. But Israel had no power to keep the law. So God gave them a "new covenant" to enable His people to live a life of obedience. We read in Jeremiah 31:33, "I will put my law in their minds, and write it on their hearts"; in 32:40, "I will put My fear in their hearts, so that they will not depart from Me"; in Ezekiel 36:27, "I will . . . cause you to walk in My statutes." These wonderful promises should give us the assurance that obedience will be their recipients' delight.

Let us listen to what the Lord Jesus says about obedience: "He who has My commandments and keeps them, it is he who loves Me. And he who loves Me will be loved by My Father, and I will love him. . . . And We will . . . make Our home with him" (John 14:21, 23). And in 15:10, "If you keep My commandments, you will abide in My love." These words are an inexhaustible treasure. Faith can firmly trust Christ to *enable us to live such a life of love and obedience.*

No father can train his children unless they are obedient. No teacher can teach a child who continues to disobey him. No general can lead his soldiers to victory without prompt obedience. Ask God to imprint this lesson on your heart: *The life of faith is a life of obedience*. As Christ lived in obedience to the Father, so we too need obedience for a life in the love of God.

Alas, the thought is too common: "I cannot be obedient, it is quite impossible." Yes, impossible to you, but not to God. He has promised to "*cause you to walk in [His] statutes*." Pray and meditate on these words, and the Holy Spirit will enlighten your eyes so that you will have power to do God's will. Let your fellowship with the Father and with the Lord Jesus Christ have as its one aim and object—a life of quiet, determined, unquestioning obedience.

Day 10

Confession of Sin

If we confess our sins, He is faithful and just to forgive us our sins and to cleanse us from all unrighteousness.

First John 1:9

TOO often the confession of sin is superficial, and often it is quite neglected. Few Christians realize how necessary it is to be in earnest about the matter, or feel that an honest confession of sin gives power to live the life of victory over sin. *In fellowship with the Lord Jesus, we need to confess with a sincere heart every sin that may be a hindrance in our Christian lives.*

Listen to what David says: "I acknowledged my sin to You, / And my iniquity I have not hidden. / I said, 'I will confess my transgressions to the Lord,' / And You forgave the iniquity of my sin. . . . You are my hiding place; / You shall preserve me from trouble; / You shall surround me with songs of deliverance" (Ps. 32:5, 7). David speaks of a time when he was unwilling to confess his sin. "When I kept silent . . . Your hand was heavy upon me" (Ps. 32:3–4). *But when he had confessed his sin, a wonderful change came.*

Confession means not only that I confess my sin with shame, but that I hand it over to God, trusting Him to take it away. Such a confession implies that I am wholly unable to get rid of my guilt, but by an act of faith I reckon on God to deliver me. This deliverance means, in the first place, that I know my sins are forgiven; and secondly, that Christ undertakes to cleanse me from the sin and keep me from its power.

O Christian, if you are seeking to have fellowship with Jesus, do not fear to confess *each sin* in the confident assurance that there is deliverance. Let there be a mutual understanding between the Lord Jesus and yourself that you will confess each sin and obtain forgiveness. Then you will know your Lord as "Jesus who saves His people from their sin." Believe that there is great *power* in the confession of sin, for the burden of sin is borne by our Lord and Savior.

Day 11

The First Love

I have this against you, that you have left your first love.
Revelation 2:4

IN Revelation 2:2–3, eight signs are mentioned showing the zeal and activity of the church at Ephesus. But there was one bad sign, and the Lord said: "Repent . . . or else I will come to you quickly and remove your lampstand from its place" (2:5). And what was this sign? "*You have left your first love.*"

We find the same lack in the church of the present day. There is zeal for the truth, there is continuous and persevering labor, but that which the Lord values most is wanting: *the tender, fervent love to Himself.*

This is a thought of great significance: A church or a community, or an individual Christian, may be an example in every good work, and yet—*the tender love for the Lord Jesus in the inner chamber is missing.*

There is no personal daily fellowship with Christ, and all the manifold activities with which people satisfy themselves are as nought in the eyes of the Master Himself.

Dear brother and sister, this little book speaks of the fellowship of love with Christ in the inner chamber. Everything depends on this. Christ came from heaven to love us with the love wherewith the Father loved Him. He suffered and died to win our hearts for this love. *His love can be satisfied with nothing less than a deep, personal love on our part.*

Christ considers this of the first importance. Let us do so too. Many ministers and missionaries and Christian workers confess with shame that in spite of all their zeal in the Lord's work, their prayer life is defective because they have left their first love. I urge you to write this down on a piece of paper and remember it continually: *The love of Jesus must be all*—in the inner chamber, in all my work, in my daily life.

Day 12

The Holy Spirit

He will glorify Me, for He will take of what is Mine and declare it to you.

John 16:14

OUR Lord, in the last night that He was with His disciples, promised to send the Holy Spirit as a helper. Although His bodily presence was removed, they would realize His presence in them and with them in a wonderful way. The Holy Spirit as God would so reveal Christ in their hearts that they would experience His presence with them continually. The Spirit would glorify Christ and would reveal the glorified Christ in heavenly love and power.

How little do Christians understand and believe and experience this glorious truth. We should fail in our duty as ministers if in a little book like this, or in our preaching, we encouraged Christians to love the Lord Jesus without at the same time warning them that it is not a duty they can perform in their own strength. No, that is impossible; it is God the Holy Spirit alone who will pour out His love in our hearts and teach us to love Christ fervently. *Through the Holy Spirit we may experience the love and abiding presence of the Lord Jesus all the day.*

But let us remember that the Spirit as God must have entire possession of us. He claims our whole heart and life. He will strengthen us with might in the inner man so that we have fellowship with Christ and keep His commandments and abide in His love.

When once we have grasped this truth we will begin to feel our deep dependence on the Holy Spirit and pray the Father to send Him in power into our hearts. The Spirit will teach us to love the Word, to meditate on it, and to keep it. He will reveal the love of Christ to us that we may love Him with a pure heart fervently. Then we shall begin to see that a life lived in the love of Christ in the midst of our daily life and distractions is a glorious possibility and a blessed reality.

Day 13

Christ's Love to Us

As the Father loved Me, I also have loved you; abide in My love.
John 15:9

IN companionship between friends and relations everything depends on their love to each other. Of what value is abundance of riches if love is lacking between husband and wife, or parents and children? And in our religion, of what value is all knowledge and zeal in God's work without the enlightenment and experience of Christ's love? (See 1 Cor. 13:1–3.) O Christians, the one thing needful in the inner chamber is to know by experience *how much Christ loves you, and to learn how you may abide and continue in that love.*

Think of what Christ says: "As the Father loved Me"—what a divine, everlasting, wonderful love!—"I also have loved you." It was the same love with which He had loved the Father and that He always bore in His heart, which He now gave into the hearts of His disciples. He yearns that this everlasting love should rest upon us, and work within us, that we may abide in it day by day. What a blessed life! Christ desires every disciple to live in the power of the selfsame love of God that He Himself experienced. My brother, do you realize that in your fellowship with Christ, in secret or in public, you are surrounded by and kept in this heavenly love? Let your desire reach out to this everlasting love. The Christ

Day 14

Our Love to Christ

. . . Jesus Christ, whom having not seen you love. Though now you do not see Him, yet believing, you rejoice with joy inexpressible and full of glory.

First Peter 1:7–8

WHAT a wonderful description of the Christian life! Here were people who had never seen Christ, and yet they truly loved Him and believed on Him, so that their hearts were filled with inexpressible joy. Such is the life of a Christian who really loves his Lord.

We have seen that the chief attribute of the Father and of the Son is love to each other and love to man. This should be the chief characteristic of the true Christian. The love of God and of Christ is poured out in his heart and becomes a well of living water, flowing forth as love to the Lord Jesus and the members of His body.

This love is not merely a blessed feeling. It is an active *principle.* It takes pleasure in doing the will of the beloved Lord. It rejoices to keep His commandments. The love of Christ to us was shown by His death on the cross; our love must be exhibited in unselfish, self-sacrificing lives. Oh, that we understood this: *In the Christian life love to Christ is everything!*

Great love will beget great faith: faith in His love to us, faith in the powerful revelations of His love in our hearts, faith that He through His love will work all His good pleasure in us.

with whom you desire fellowship longs inexpressibly to fill you with His love.

Read from time to time what God's Word says about the love of Christ. Meditate on the words and let them sink into your heart. Sooner or later you will begin to realize: The greatest happiness of my life is that I am beloved of the Lord Jesus. I may live in fellowship with Him all the day long.

Let your heart continually say: His love to me is inexpressible. He will keep me abiding in His love.

The wings of faith and love will lift us up to heaven, and we shall be filled with joy inexpressible. The joy of the Christian is an indispensable witness to the world of the power of Christ to change hearts and fill them with heavenly love and gladness.

O you lovers of the Lord Jesus, take time daily in the inner chamber with Him anew to drink in His heavenly love. It will make you strong in faith, and your joy will be full. Love, joy, faith—these will be our life each day through the grace of our Lord Jesus.

Day 15

Love to the Brethren

A new commandment I give to you, that you love one another; as I have loved you, that you also love one another. . . . that you love one another as I have loved you.

John 13:34; 15:12

THE Lord Jesus told His disciples that as the Father had loved Him, even so He loved them. And now, following His example, we must love one another with the same love. "By this all will know that you are My disciples, if you have love for one another" (13:35). He had prayed, "That they all may be one, as You, Father, are in Me, and I in You; that they also may be one in Us, that the world may believe that You sent Me" (17:21). If we exhibit the love that was in God toward Christ, and in Christ to us, the world will be obliged to confess that our Christianity is genuine and from above.

This is what actually happened. The Greeks and Romans, Jews and heathen, hated each other. Among all the nations of the world there was hardly a thought of love to each other. The very idea of self-sacrifice was a strange one. When the heathen saw that Christians from different nations, under the powerful working of the Holy Spirit, became one, and loved one another—even to the point of self-sacrifice in time of plague or illness—they were amazed and said: "Behold how these people love one another!"

Day 16

Love to Souls

Know that he who turns a sinner from the error of his way will save a soul from death and cover a multitude of sins.

James 5:20

WHAT a wonderful thought—that I may save a soul from everlasting death! How can this be? If I turn him from the error of his ways. This is the calling not only of the minister but of every Christian—*to work for the salvation of sinners.*

When Christ and His love took possession of our hearts, He gave us this love that we might bring others to Him. In this way Christ's kingdom is being extended. Everyone who has the love of Christ in his heart should be constrained to tell others. This was the case in the early Christian church. After the day of Pentecost, people went out and told of the love of Christ which they had themselves experienced. Heathen writers have told us that the rapid spread of Christianity in the first century was due to the fact that each convert, being filled with the love of Christ, tried to bring the good news to others.

What a change has come over the church! Many Christians never try to win others to Christ. Their love is so weak and faint that they have no desire to help others. May the time soon come when Christians will feel constrained to tell of the love of Christ. In a revival in Korea a few years ago, the converts were filled with

Among professing Christians there is a certain oneness of belief and feeling of brotherhood, but Christ's heavenly love is often lacking and we do not bear one another's burdens or love others heartily.

Pray that you may love your fellow believers with the same love with which Christ loved you. If we abide in Christ's love and let that love fill our hearts, supernatural power will be given us to take all God's children to our hearts in love. As close as is the bond of love between the Father and the Son, between Christ and His followers, so close must the bond of love be between all God's children.

such a burning love to Christ that they felt bound to tell others of His love. It was even taken as a test of membership that each one should have brought another to the Lord before being admitted to the church.

Let the reader examine himself and pray that, in fellowship with Christ, he may think not only of his own soul but, having received the gift of God's love, he may pass it on to others. He will then know true happiness, the joy of bringing souls to Christ.

Let us pray earnestly to be so *filled* with God's love that we may wholeheartedly surrender ourselves to win others for Him.

Day 17

The Spirit of Love

The love of God has been poured out in our hearts by the Holy Spirit who was given to us.

Romans 5:5

The fruit of the Spirit is love.

Galatians 5:22

THE thought sometimes arises, as we consider Christ's love to us, our love to Christ, our love to the brethren or to souls around us: The demand is too great, it is unattainable, it is impossible for a Christian to live this life of love, and to show it to the brethren and to needy souls. And because we deem it impossible, and because of our unbelief and lack of faith in God's promises, we make little progress in this spirit of love.

We need continually to remind ourselves that it is not in our own strength, or even by serious thought, that we can attain to the love of Christ. We must realize the truth that the love of God is poured out in our hearts and will be poured out afresh daily by *the Spirit of God.* It is only as we are wholly surrendered to the leading of the Spirit that we will be able to live according to God's will. When the inner life of love is renewed day by day, we shall feel compelled to work for souls.

Here is a prayer from Scripture that you and I can appropriately offer: "I bow my knees to the Father . . . that He would grant you . . . to be strengthened with might through His Spirit in the inner man, that Christ may dwell in your hearts through faith; that you, *being rooted and grounded in love, may . . . know the love of Christ which passes knowledge*" (Eph. 3:14–19). Yes, it is our privilege to be rooted and grounded in this love and personally know the love that passes knowledge—but on one condition: *We must be strengthened by the Spirit in the inner man, so that Christ may dwell in our heart.* Then it is that we will indeed be rooted and grounded in love.

Christian, take this message from God's Word and let it influence your life. Unless you wait upon God daily on your knees for His Spirit to be revealed in your heart, you cannot live in this love. A life of prayer will make a life in the love of Christ, in the love of the brethren, in love to souls, a blessed reality in your experience.

Put your confidence privately each day in the Holy Spirit—the Spirit of love whom God will give to those who ask in faith.

Day 18

Persevering Prayer

Men always ought to pray and not lose heart.

Luke 18:1

Continuing steadfastly in prayer.

Romans 12:12

Pray without ceasing.

First Thessalonians 5:17

ONE of the greatest drawbacks to the life of prayer is the fact that the answer does not come as speedily as we expect. We can be discouraged by the thought *Perhaps I am praying wrongly*, and so we do not persevere in prayer.

Perseverance: This was a lesson that our Lord taught often and urgently. If we consider the matter we can see that there may be a reason for God's delay, and the waiting may bring a blessing to our souls. Our desire must grow deeper and stronger, and we must ask with our whole heart. God puts us into the practicing school of persevering prayer so that our weak faith may be strengthened. Do believe that there is a great blessing in the delayed answer to prayer.

Above all, God would draw us into closer fellowship with Himself. When our prayers are not answered, we learn to realize that the fellowship and nearness and love of God are more to us than the answers to our petitions, and we continue in prayer. What a blessing Jacob received through the delay in the answer to his prayer! He saw God face to face, and as a prince he had power with God and prevailed.

Christians, listen to this warning. Be not impatient or discouraged if the answer does not come. "Continue steadfastly in prayer." "Pray without ceasing." You will find it an inexpressible blessing to do so. You will ask whether your prayer is really in accordance with the will of God and the Word of God. You will inquire if it is in the right spirit and in the name of Christ. Keep on praying; you will learn that the delay in the answer to prayer is one of the most precious means of grace that God can bestow on you. You will learn, too, that those who have persevered often and long before God, in pleading *His promises,* are those who have had the greatest power with God in prayer.

Day 19

The Prayer Meeting

These all continued with one accord in prayer and supplication. . . . And they were all filled with the Holy Spirit.

Acts 1:14; 2:4

(See also Matthew 18:19–20)

GREAT is the value of a genuine prayer meeting. There God's children meet together, not as in church to listen to one speaker, but to lift up their hearts unitedly to God. By this means Christians are drawn closer to each other. Those who are weak are strengthened and encouraged by the testimony of the older and more experienced members, and even young Christians have the opportunity of telling of the joy of the Lord.

The prayer meeting may become a great power for good in a congregation and a spiritual help to both minister and members. By means of intercession God's blessing is poured out at home and abroad.

But there are also dangers to be considered. Many attend, and are edified, but never learn to pray themselves. Others go for the sake of social and religious fervor, and have a form of godliness but do not know the hidden life of prayer. Unless there is *much and earnest prayer in the inner chamber*, attendance at a prayer meeting may be a mere form.

It is well to ask: What constitutes a living prayer meeting?

For a prayer meeting to have its optimal effect, there needs to be hearty love and fellowship between those in attendance. The leaders should realize how great the influence of such a meeting may be, especially when its roots are nourished by the life of prayer in the inner chamber. Prayer items should include God's people and ministries all over the world, not personal and local needs alone. And above all, as on the day of Pentecost, there must be waiting on God for the filling with the Holy Spirit. He must be in control.

Dear reader, this little book aims at helping you in your personal spiritual life. But remember, you do not live for yourself alone, but are part of the body of Christ. Your prayer, wherever you are, must include in its intercession all Christians. As the roots of the tree hidden deep in the earth and the branches spread out to heaven are one, so the *hidden* prayer life is inseparably bound up with *united* prayer.

Day 20

Intercession

Praying always . . . in the Spirit . . . with all perseverance and supplication for all the saints.

Ephesians 6:18

WHAT an inexpressible blessing there is in intercession. That one should pray down heavenly gifts on himself is a wonder of grace, but that he should bring down blessings on others is indeed an inconceivable honor. Will God indeed make the pouring out of blessing on others *dependent on our prayers*? Yes, He makes us His remembrancers and fellow workers. He has taken us into partnership in His work; if we fail in doing our part, others will suffer, and His work will suffer inexpressible loss.

God has appointed intercession as one of the means by which souls shall be saved and saints and ministers of the gospel edified and built up in the faith. Even the ends of the earth will receive life and blessing through our prayers. Should we not expect God's children to strive joyfully and with all their powers, by means of intercession, to bring down blessing on the world?

Christian, begin to use intercession as a means of grace for yourself and for others. Pray for your neighbors. Pray for souls with the definite desire that they may be won for Christ. Pray for your minister, for all ministers and missionaries. Pray for your country and people, for rulers and subjects. Pray for all men. If you surrender yourself to the guidance of the Holy Spirit and live a life wholly for God, you will realize that the time spent in praying is an offering well pleasing to God, bringing blessing to yourself and power into the lives of those for whom you pray.

Yes, "[pray] always with all prayer and supplication . . . being watchful . . . with all perseverance and supplication for all the saints." And in so doing you will learn the lesson that intercession is the chief means of winning souls and bringing glory to God.

Day 21

Prayer and Fasting

So Jesus said to them, "Because of your unbelief [you were unable]. . . . However, this kind does not go out except by prayer and fasting."

Matthew 17:20–21

OUR Lord here teaches us that a life of faith requires both prayer and fasting. That is, prayer grasps the power of heaven, fasting loosens the hold on earthly pleasure.

Jesus Himself fasted to get strength to resist the devil. He taught His disciples that even as with prayer and almsgiving, fasting should be in secret, and that the heavenly Father would reward openly. Abstinence from food, or temperance in taking it, helps to strengthen the soul for fellowship with God.

Let us learn this great lesson that abstinence, temperance, and self-denial in temporal things is a help to the spiritual life. After having partaken of a hearty meal, one does not feel much desire to pray. To willingly sacrifice our own pleasure or bodily enjoyment, and to subdue the lust of the flesh and the lust of the eyes, will help to set our minds more fully on heavenly things. The very exertion needed in overcoming the desires of the flesh will give us strength to take hold of God in prayer.

The great lesson is this: Our dullness in prayer comes from our fleshly desire for comfort and ease. "Those who are Christ's have crucified the flesh with its passions and desires" (Gal. 5:24). Prayer is no easy work. It may easily become a mere form. For the real practice of prayer—taking hold of God and having communion with Him—it is necessary that all that can please the flesh must be sacrificed and given over to death.

Beloved Christian, do believe that it is worth any trouble to deny ourselves daily in order to meet the Holy God and receive from Him heavenly blessings.

Day 22

The Spirit of Prayer

The Spirit . . . makes intercession for the saints.
Romans 8:27

PRAYER is not our work but God's work, which He works within us by His almighty power. As we think of this, our attitude should be one of silent expectation that, as we pray, the Holy Spirit shall help our infirmities and pray within us with groanings too deep for words.

What a thought! When I feel how defective my prayer is, when I have no strength of my own, I may bow in silence before God in the confidence that His Holy Spirit will teach me to pray. The Spirit is the Spirit of prayer. It is not my work, but God's work in me. My very desire is a sign that God will hear me. When God would grant our requests, He first works the desire in our hearts; and the Spirit will perfect the work, even in our weakness. We see this in the story of Jacob. The same One who wrestled with him and seemed to withhold the blessing was in reality strengthening him to *continue* and to *prevail* in prayer. What a wondrous thought! Prayer is the work of the triune God: the Father, who wakens the desire and will give all we need; the Son, who through His intercession teaches us to pray in His name; and the Holy Spirit, who in secret will strengthen our feeble desires.

We have spoken of the Spirit of truth who will glorify Christ in us, and of the Spirit of love who will pour out His love in our hearts. And now we have the Spirit of prayer, through whom our life may be one of continual prayer. *Thank God! The Spirit has been given from heaven to dwell in our hearts, and to teach us to pray.*

Christian, listen to the leading of the Spirit. Obey His voice in all things. He will make you a man of prayer. You will then realize the glory of your calling as intercessor—asking great things of God for those around you, for the church, and for the whole heathen world.

Day 23

Wholly for Christ

He died for all, that those who live should live no longer for themselves, but for Him who died for them and rose again.
Second Corinthians 5:15

HERE we have three lives mentioned and described. First, the life of the Christian who lives according to his old nature: *he lives for himself alone*. Second, the life of the true Christian: *he lives wholly for Christ*. Third, the life of Christ in heaven: *He lives wholly for us*.

Many a Christian needs to be convinced of the folly of living only for himself. At conversion he thinks mostly about his own salvation and less about the glory of God and the right that Christ, who has redeemed us with His precious blood, has concerning him. Many Christians just live for themselves, content with doing a little for the Master. Happy is the believer who realizes his high calling and the privilege and blessedness of consecrating his life entirely to God's service.

The great hindrance to such a life is the unbelief which says it is impossible. But when the truth takes hold of us—Christ in heaven lives wholly for *me*, will impart *His life* to me, and will enable me to live wholly for *Him*—then we will be able to say joyfully: "Dear Lord Jesus, from this moment let my prayer each day be: *Wholly for Christ . . . Wholly for Christ*."

Dear brother, let nothing less be your earnest desire, your prayer, and your firm expectation. Christ has not only died for you but lives in heaven to keep and sanctify you, His purchased possession. Ponder this wonderful thought—that Christ will keep you as a member of His body, to work and live for Him. Pray for grace to live wholly for God, in seeking souls and in serving His people. Take time day by day to be so united to Christ in the inner man that you can say with all your heart: "I live wholly for Him who gave Himself wholly for me . . . and who now lives in heaven wholly for me."

Day 24

The Cross of Christ

I have been crucified with Christ.

Galatians 2:20

THE cross of Christ is His greatest glory. Because He humbled Himself to the death of the cross, *therefore* God has highly exalted Him. The cross was the power that conquered Satan and sin.

The Christian shares with Christ in the cross. The crucified Christ lives in him through the Holy Spirit, and the spirit of the cross inspires him. He lives as one who has died with Christ. As he realizes the power of Christ's crucifixion, he lives as one who has died to the world and to sin, and the power becomes a reality in his life. It is as the *Crucified One* that Christ lives in me.

Our Lord said to His disciples: "Take up the cross, and follow Me" (Mark 10:21). Did they understand this? They had seen men carrying a cross and they knew what it meant: a painful death lay just ahead. All His life Christ bore His cross—the death sentence that He should die for the world. And each Christian must bear his cross, acknowledging that he is worthy of death and believing that he is crucified with Christ and that the Crucified One lives in him. "Our old man was crucified with [Christ]" (Rom. 6:6). "Those who are Christ's have crucified the flesh with its passions and desires" (Gal. 5:24). When we have accepted this life of the cross we will be able to say with Paul: "God forbid that I should boast except in the cross of our Lord Jesus Christ" (Gal. 6:14).

This is a deep spiritual truth. Think and pray over it, and the Holy Spirit will teach you. Let the disposition of Christ on the cross—His humility, His sacrifice of all worldly honor, His spirit of self-denial—take possession of you. The power of His death will work in you, and you will become like Him in His death—for you will know Him and the power of His resurrection. Take time, O soul, that Christ through His Spirit may reveal Himself as the Crucified One.

Day 25

The World

Do not love the world or the things in the world. If anyone loves the world, the love of the Father is not in him.

First John 2:15

JOHN teaches us clearly what he means by the world. He says: "All that is in the world—the lust of the flesh, the lust of the eyes, and the pride of life—is not of the Father but is of the world" (2:16).

The world is that disposition or power under which man has fallen through sin. And the god of this world, in order to deceive man, conceals himself under the form of what God has created. The world with its pleasures surrounds the Christian each day with temptations.

This was the case with Eve in the garden of Eden. We find in Genesis 3:6 the three characteristics which John mentions: (1) the lust of the flesh—"The woman saw that the tree was good for food," (2) the lust of the eyes—"It was pleasant to the eyes," (3) the pride of life—"a tree desirable to make one wise." And the world still comes to us offering desirable food, and much else, to please the fleshly appetites. And much that the eye desires: riches and beauty and luxury. And the pride of life: when a man imagines he knows and understands everything, and prides himself on it. Is our life in the world not full of danger, what with the allurements of the flesh which so much occupy our eyes and our hearts, and so much worldly wisdom and knowledge?

So John tells us: "Do not love the world, for then the love of the Father is not in you." And our Lord calls us, as He called His disciples of old, to leave all and follow Him.

Christian, you live in a dangerous world! Cleave fast to the Lord Jesus. As He teaches you to shun the world and its attractions, your love will go out to Him in loyal-hearted service. But remember—there must be daily fellowship with Jesus. His love *alone* can expel the love of the world. Take time to be alone with your Lord.

Day 26

Put On Christ

As many of you as were baptized
into Christ have put on Christ.

Galatians 3:27

Put on the Lord Jesus Christ, and make no
provision for the flesh, to fulfill its lusts.

Romans 13:14

THE word that is here translated "put on" is the same that is used in regard to putting on clothes. We have put on "the new man," and we have the new nature as a *garment* that is worn, by means of which all can see who we are.

Paul says of the Christian that when he has confessed Christ at baptism, he has put on Christ. As a man may be recognized by the garment he wears, so the Christian is known as one who has put on Christ—exhibits Him in his whole life and character.

And again he says: "Put on the Lord Jesus." Not at conversion alone but day by day. As I put on my clothes each day and am seen in them, so the Christian must daily put on the Lord Jesus—so that he no longer lives after the flesh to fulfill its lusts but shows forth the image of his Lord, even the new man formed in His likeness.

Put on Christ! This work must be done each day in the inner chamber. I must put on the Lord, the heavenly Jesus. But I need time to put on Christ. As my garments cover me and protect me from wind and sun, even so Christ Jesus will be my beauty, my defense, and my joy. As I commune with Him in prayer He imparts Himself to me, and strengthens me to walk as one who is in Him and bound to Him forever.

O soul, take time to meditate on this wonderful truth. Just as your clothing is a necessity as you go out into the world, let it be equally indispensable for you to put on Jesus Christ, to abide in Him and walk with Him all the day.

You feel that this cannot be done hastily and superficially. Rightly so. It takes time, quiet time in living fellowship with Jesus, to realize that you have put Him on. Take the time and the trouble. Your reward will be great.

The Strength of the Christian

Finally, my brethren, be strong in the Lord and in the power of His might.

Ephesians 6:10

THE apostle has reached the end of his epistle, and begins his last division with the words: "Finally, my brethren, be strong in the Lord." The Christian needs strength. This we all know. The Christian has no strength of his own. This is also true. Where may strength be obtained? Notice the answer: "Be strong *in the Lord* and in the power of His might."

Paul had spoken of this power in the earlier part of his epistle (1:17–19). He had prayed God to give them the Spirit so that they might know the exceeding greatness of His power—according to the working of His mighty power which He wrought in Christ when He raised Him from the dead. This is the literal truth: *The exceeding greatness of His power*, which raised Christ from the dead, *works in every believer!* In me and in you, my reader. We hardly believe it. That is why Paul prays—and we must pray with him—that God through His Spirit would teach us to believe in His almighty power. Pray with all your heart: "Father, grant me the Spirit of wisdom, that I may experience this power in my life."

In 3:16–17, Paul prays the Father to grant them, according to the riches of His glory, to be strengthened with might by His Spirit in the inner man, that Christ might dwell in their hearts. And then: "Now to Him who is able to do exceedingly abundantly above all that we ask or think, *according to the power that works in us*, to Him be glory" (Eph. 3:20–21).

Read over these two passages again, and pray for God's Spirit to enlighten your eyes. Believe in the divine power working within you. Pray that the Holy Spirit may reveal it to you, and appropriate the promise that God will manifest His power in your heart, supplying all your needs.

Do you not begin to realize that time is needed—much time in communion with the Father and the Son—if you would experience the power of God within you?

Day 28

The Whole Heart

With my whole heart I have sought You; Oh, let me not wander from Your commandments!

Psalm 119:10

NOTICE how often the psalmist speaks here of the whole heart. "Those . . . who seek Him with the whole heart" (119:2). "I shall observe [Your law] with my whole heart" (119:34). "I will keep Your precepts with my whole heart" (119:69). "I cry out with my whole heart" (119:145). In seeking God, in observing His law, in crying out for His help—each time it is with the whole heart.

When we want to make anything a success in worldly affairs, we put our whole heart into it. And is this not much more necessary in the service of a holy God? Is He not worthy? Does not His great holiness and the natural aversion of our hearts from God demand it? The whole heart is needed in the service of God when we worship Him in secret.

And yet how little most Christians think of this. They do not remember how necessary it is—in prayer, in reading God's Word, in striving to do His will—to say continually: *With my whole heart I have sought You.* Yes, when we pray, and when we try to understand God's Word and to obey His commands, let us say: I desire to seek God, to serve Him, and to please Him with my whole heart.

"With my whole heart I have sought You." Dear reader, take this word into your heart. Think over it. Pray over it. Speak it out before God until you feel: I really mean what I say, and I have the assurance that God will hear my prayer. Say it each morning as you approach God in prayer: "I seek You with my whole heart." You will by degrees feel the need of waiting in holy stillness upon God that He may take possession of your whole heart, and you will learn to love Him with your whole heart and with all your strength.

In Christ

Of [God] you are in Christ Jesus.

First Corinthians 1:30

THE expression "in Christ" is often used in the Epistles. The Christian cannot read God's Word aright, nor experience its full power in his life, until he prayerfully and believingly accepts this truth: *I am in Christ Jesus.*

The Lord Jesus, in the last night with His disciples, used an equivalent expression several times. "At that day"—when the Spirit has been poured out—"you will know that I am in My Father, and *you in Me*" (John 14:20). And then follows, "*Abide in Me*. . . . He who abides *in Me* . . . bears much fruit" (15:4–5). "If you abide *in Me* . . . you will ask what you desire, and it shall be done for you" (15:7). But the Christian cannot appropriate these promises unless he first prayerfully accepts the word: *in Christ.*

Paul expresses the same thought in Romans. "We were buried with [Christ]" (6:4). "[We are] dead indeed to sin, but alive to God in Christ Jesus" (6:11). "There is . . . no condemnation to those who are in Christ Jesus" (8:1). And in Ephesians: "God . . . has blessed us with every spiritual blessing . . . in Christ" (1:3), "chose us in Him" (1:4), and "made us accepted in the Beloved" (1:6). "In Him we have redemption" (1:7). And in

Colossians: "In Him dwells all the fullness" (2:9). We are "perfect in Christ Jesus" (1:28). "Walk in Him" (2:6). "You are complete in Him" (2:10).

Let our faith take hold of the words: "[God] establishes us . . . in Christ" (2 Cor. 1:21). "Of [God I am] in Christ Jesus" (1 Cor. 1:30). The Holy Spirit will make it our experience. Pray earnestly and follow the leading of the Spirit. The word will take root in your heart, and you will realize something of its heavenly power. But remember that abiding in Christ is a matter of the heart. It must be cultivated in a spirit of love. Only as we take time day by day in fellowship with Christ will the abiding in Christ become a blessed reality, and the inner man will be renewed day by day.

Day 30

Christ in Me

Do you not know . . . that Jesus Christ is in you?
Second Corinthians 13:5

THE apostle would have each Christian live in the full assurance: Christ is in me. What a difference it would make in our lives if we could take time every morning to be filled with the thought: Christ is in me. *As assuredly as I am in Christ, Christ is also in me.*

In the last night, Christ put it clearly to His disciples that the Spirit would teach them: "At that day you will know that I am in My Father, and you in Me, and I *in you*" (John 14:20). First of all, *you are in Me.* Through the power of God, all we who believe were crucified with Christ and raised again with Him. And as a result: *Christ is in us.* But this knowledge does not come easily. Through faith in God's Word the Christian accepts it, and the Holy Spirit will lead us into all truth. Take time this very day to realize and appropriate this blessing in prayer.

How clearly Paul expresses the thought in the prayer of Ephesians 3:16–17: "That [the Father] would grant you, according to the riches of His glory . . ." Notice that it is not the ordinary gift of grace, but a special revelation of the riches of His love and power which is here being invoked. That He grant you "to be strengthened with might through His Spirit in the inner man, *that Christ may dwell in your hearts through faith*" (Eph. 3:16–17). Have you grasped it? The Christian may really have the experience of being filled with the fullness of God.

Dear Christian, Paul said: "I bow my knees to the Father" (3:14). That is the only way to obtain the blessing. Take time in the inner chamber to realize: *Christ dwells in me.* Too little have I experienced this in the past, but I will cry to God and wait upon Him to *perfect* His work in me. Even in the midst of my daily work I must look upon my heart as the dwelling place of the Son of God, and say: "*I am* crucified with Christ, I live no more; *Christ lives in me.*" Thus only will Christ's words "Abide in Me, and I in you" (John 15:4) become my daily experience.

Day 31

Christ Is All

Christ is all and in all.

Colossians 3:11

IN the eternal counsel of God, in the redemption on the cross, as King on the throne in heaven and on earth—*Christ is all!* In the salvation of sinners, in their justification and sanctification, in the upbuilding of Christ's body, in the care for individuals—even the most sinful—this word avails: *Christ is all.* Every day and every hour it affords comfort and strength to the child of God who accepts it in faith: *Christ is all.*

Have you perhaps thought in reading these pages that the full salvation here described is not meant for you? You feel too weak, too unworthy, too untrustworthy. My dear reader, do believe that if you will only accept the Lord Jesus in childlike faith, you have a leader and a guide who will supply all your need. Believe with your whole heart in the word of our Savior, "Lo, I am with you always" (Matt. 28:20), and you will experience His presence each day. However cold and dull your feelings may be, however sinful you are, meet the Lord Jesus in secret and He will reveal Himself to you. Tell Him how wretched you are, and then trust Him to help and sustain you. Wait before Him until by faith you can rejoice in Him. Read this little book over again, and read it with the thought: Christ is all. I have failed to remember this, but each day as I go to secret prayer let this thought be with me: Christ is all. Let me take it as my motto. Whether for teaching me to pray, to strengthen my faith, to give me the assurance of His love and of access to the Father, or to make me strong for the work of the day: *Christ is all.* Yes, Christ, my Christ, is all I need. This truth will teach me to abide in His love. It will give me the assurance that He dwells in my heart, and that I may know the love that passes knowledge. God be praised to all eternity: Christ, my Christ, is my all in all!

CLC PUBLICATIONS

Fort Washington, PA 19034

This book is published by CLC Publications, an outreach of CLC Ministries International. The purpose of CLC is to make evangelical Christian literature available to all nations so that people may come to faith and maturity in the Lord Jesus Christ. We hope this book has been life changing and has enriched your walk with God through the work of the Holy Spirit. If you would like to know more about CLC, we invite you to visit our website:
www.clcusa.org

To know more about the remarkable story of the founding of CLC International we encourage you to read

LEAP OF FAITH

Norman Grubb

Paperback
Size 5¼ x 8, Pages 248
ISBN: 978-0-87508-650-7
ISBN (e-book): 978-1-61958-055-8

THE SECRET OF ADORATION

Andrew Murray

The Secret Series books contain a wealth of teaching that is based on Andrew Murray's mature and full experience in Christ. *The Secret of Adoration* contains one month of daily selections that highlight the importance of true worship in the lives of believers.

Paperback
Size $4^{1}/_{4}$ x 7, Pages 71
ISBN: 978-1-61958-253-8
ISBN (*e-book*): 978-1-61958-254-5